Enjoying
EXMOOR

HILARY BINDING

**EXMOOR
BOOKS**

First published in 1999

BRITISH LIBRARY CATALOGUING IN PUBLICATION DATA
A catalogue record for this book is available from The British Library

ISBN 0 86183 425 9

EXMOOR BOOKS
Dulverton, Somerset

Trade sales enquiries:
Halsgrove, Halsgrove House,
Lower Moor Way, Tiverton, Devon EX16 6SS
Tel: 01884 243242 Fax: 01884 243325 www.halsgrove.com

Exmoor Books is a partnership between Exmoor Press
and Exmoor National Park Authority

Printed by UIC Printing and Packaging Pte Ltd, Singapore

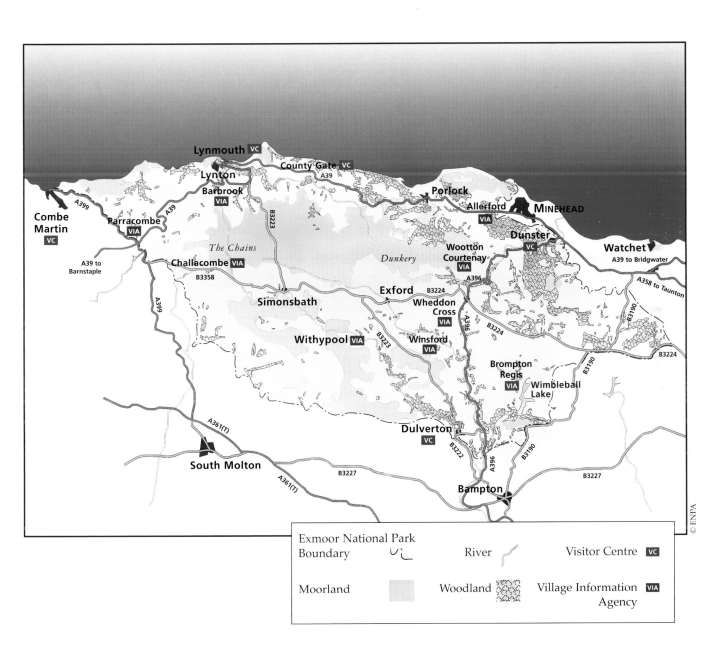

Combe Martin VC
A399
A39 to Barnstaple
Parracombe VIA
A39
Lynmouth VC
Lynton
Barbrook VIA
County Gate VC
A39
Porlock
Allerford VIA
MINEHEAD
Dunster VC
Watchet
A39 to Bridgwater
A358 to Taunton
The Chains
Challacombe VIA
B3358
B3223
Dunkery
Wootton Courtenay VIA
Simonsbath
Exford
B3224
Wheddon Cross VIA
A396
A396
B3224
Withypool VIA
B3223
Winsford VIA
A396
B3190
Brompton Regis VIA
Wimbleball Lake
B3190
B3224
A399
A361(T)
South Molton
A361(T)
B3227
Dulverton VC
B3222
A396
B3190
Bampton
B3227

© ENPA

Exmoor National Park Boundary | River | Visitor Centre VC

Moorland | Woodland | Village Information Agency VIA

E. R. J. Davey

FOREWORD

Enjoying Exmoor is a wonderful read for anyone who plans to visit Exmoor. It is written in a friendly style with a ready reference layout and many excellent pictures.

I have lived on a remote hill farm in the epicentre of Exmoor National Park for fifteen years and still find the Exmoor views more satisfying and colourful, whatever the season, than any other landscape I can remember.

This book describes the special character and appeal of Exmoor's scenery from rugged coastline to high moorland, from deep valley villages to Roman fortlets. You can learn where to go to see Red Deer, herds of Exmoor Ponies and, with luck, a good many other wild animals and birds.

There are alphabetical lists of interesting villages, historic sites and the best places to take the family as well as sections high-lighting museums, Exmoor crafts, customs and local food and drink, with a map and symbols in the text providing an easy guide to available amenities.

For visitors interested in local history an outline description of man's impact on Exmoor is given stretching back to 6800BC which reminds us how Somerset Romans guarded the coast against marauding Welshmen from over the Bristol Channel.

There is an excellent network of bus services on Exmoor. There is no need to use your car for every outing when you can take advantage of one of the many buses or join a Land Rover tour with a guide who knows where to go and how best to see the superb views and wildlife. Remote waterfalls, wild moorland footpaths, evocative ruins, farm walks, tiny coastal churches reachable only on foot, lakes with facilities for fishing and sailing, where to hire bicycles and ponies, the best routes for walking, trekking or biking with or without a guide are all featured. There are details on where to go boating, surfing, swimming or simply how to view Exmoor's most lovely woods and heather vistas. And much more.

Enjoying Exmoor is designed to help visitors enjoy their visit to the full. It is also hoped that the book will encourage everyone to help look after this beautiful and fragile landscape which has so far survived largely unspoilt in our crowded island.

Sir Ranulph Fiennes Bt, OBE

Riding at Horner

CONTENTS

Early morning mist near Dulverton.

INTRODUCTION

There are few places in England – some would say the world! – that have such a variety of beautiful, unspoilt scenery packed into such a relatively small space as Exmoor. Heather and grass moorland contrasts with deep wooded valleys; tiny rushing streams come together to form fast-flowing rivers; high cliffs cut by steep ravines give way to wide pebble beaches and secure harbours. Ancient farms shelter on the slopes of hills surrounded by green hedged fields, while isolated scatterings of cob-and-thatch cottages cling to the security of their tiny white-washed churches and chapels. Larger villages, small towns even, buzz with the traditional business of buying and selling, providing for the needs of local people and visitors. It is a wonderful place for a holiday!

Fifty years ago it was realised that Exmoor's landscape was unique and that steps should be taken to ensure that it was not spoilt by intrusive developments but preserved for people to enjoy for ever. Because of this Exmoor was made a National Park, one of eleven in England and Wales. Over the years ideas have changed but Exmoor National Park Authority is still working to balance the needs of the people who live in the Park with those of visitors and of the landscape itself.

The Authority doesn't try to look after Exmoor on its own but works alongside the people whose homes and jobs are in the Park. After all, Exmoor today is like it is because of the way people have used it in the past and its future depends on how it is treated now by visitors as well as by local people. The Park Authority firmly believes that the more people get to know, understand and enjoy Exmoor the more they will want to help look after it.

This book is designed to give you a flavour of Exmoor; its history, its habitats, its wildlife, as well as suggesting places to visit, walks to take and things to do. The best places to provide you with more information about Exmoor are the five National Park Visitor Centres. You can find out where they are on page 62.

E. R. J. Davey

Brian Preace

Clockwise from top left:

Learning about Exmoor with Ranger Alison.

Brompton Regis, a thriving community in the Brendon Hills.

Volunteers help with maintaining footpaths.

Traditional beech hedges.

EXMOOR NATIONAL PARK AUTHORITY'S JOB IS TO:

- Firstly, conserve and enhance the natural beauty, wildlife and cultural heritage of the Park.
- Secondly, promote opportunities for the understanding and enjoyment of the special qualities of the Park by the public.
- And, while pursuing these two objectives, to foster the social and economic well-being of the communities living within the Park.

GIVE YOUR CAR A HOLIDAY!

Most visitors to Exmoor come by car and use it for getting around the National Park during their stay. But despite its comfort and convenience the car can cause problems for the environment, for other road users and pedestrians and even for the owner! Trying to find a parking space in a popular place and being held-up in slow-moving traffic, for example, can be very stressful.

For some, such as the elderly and infirm, or disabled people, the car may be the only way to see and enjoy Exmoor. For others, however, there is an alternative and that is to travel by bus. Buses relieve the visitor of worries about parking, take away the stress of driving, and provide a much better view than the car – and the car driver can relax and enjoy the scenery as well!

From around the end of May until the end of September there are good bus services which enable you to get to most places on Exmoor and can be used for a full or half day out. There are also some bus services at other times of the year and these are on the increase. If you're not sure where to go, staff at the ENP Visitor Centres and

Village Information Agencies will be glad to help you plan a route.

Details of all the bus services on and around Exmoor can be found in the *Exmoor and West Somerset Public Transport Guide* which is published by the National Park Authority and is available, free of charge, from ENP Visitor Centres and Village Information Agencies, Tourist Information Centres as well as local shops, guest houses, hotels and libraries. The guide gives the routes and times of all services and also provides ideas for walks using the bus. Other leaflets are also available giving ideas for places to visit, which buses to use, where to catch them and so on.

Some places, like Dunster, Lynton and Lynmouth, and Tarr Steps get very busy at the height of the season. If you have to use the car its a good idea to go early or late in the day to avoid the crowds. Its also important to remember that small, local roads are used by farmers moving stock or machinery as well as by riders, cyclists and walkers, so extra care should be taken when driving.

PEOPLE AND THE MOOR

Cow Castle – an Iron Age hill fort.

The earliest traces of people on Exmoor go back to about 6800 BC after the last ice age. As the ice melted and the land warmed up again, plants and animals colonised the area, and, in pursuit of these important sources of food, people began to use Exmoor as a summer hunting ground. They lived in camps near springs, hunted deer and other animals, gathered plants and berries and made and repaired their flint tools and weapons. In winter they went down to the lowlands to collect seafood and avoid the harsh weather higher up.

The vegetation in the prehistoric period on Exmoor was mainly broadleaf woodland which, as people learnt to till the ground for growing crops and to rear animals for meat, hides and wool, was gradually felled to provide clearings for fields and pastures. The remains of their houses, fields and ponds survive on the moor. Circular banks of stone formed the foundations of houses, which would have had timber, wattle or turf walls and turf or thatched roofs. Long low banks of stone are the remains of field banks and boundaries, which probably had hedges or fences along their tops. It is likely that some of the hedgebanks with beech trees on them which we see today, follow courses thousands of years old.

Mounds of earth and stone, known as barrows, often on the highest point of hills and along ridges are the tombs of people who died as long as four thousand years ago. Their size and dominating positions in the landscape suggest that they were the tombs of VIPs in the prehistoric community of Exmoor. There are many groups of these barrows on Exmoor – Wambarrows on Winsford Hill (SS 876 343) and Five Barrows near Simonsbath (SS 733 367) are easy to visit.

Huge banks and ditches, usually enclosing a circular area of ground provided meeting and trading places for the locality in the late prehistoric and Romano-British period. Their position on easily-defended vantage points suggests they were also places of safety during times of attack or unrest. Bats Castle above Dunster (SS 988 422) is an example. Further east in Wessex, Iron Age tribes defended such hillforts against Roman invaders.

On the North Devon coast of Exmoor there are two Roman fortlets, built and used between AD 50 and AD 70 as lookout posts for garrisons of 80 soldiers watching

The Ermine Street Guard at Old Burrow Roman fortlet.

ENPA

across the Bristol Channel for signs of attack from the tribes of South Wales. At Old Burrow (SS 788 494) the soldiers lived in leather tents throughout the year, a damp and chilly experience for men recruited from the Mediterranean!

Farming became the main way of life on Exmoor, with sheep rearing and wool production developing as a major industry. The farmsteads, fulling mills, packhorse bridges crossing rivers and the yarn market at Dunster illustrate the processes of the medieval and later wool trade on Exmoor.

In the nineteenth century Exmoor had its own industrial revolution when iron, which had been mined and processed for nearly two thousand years on Exmoor, and other metals were exploited on a large scale. The complex of mines, engine houses and the railway built along the Brendon Hills, with its incline down the hillside to Comberow to take the iron ore to the port of Watchet, was in operation in the second part of the century. The influx of miners and engineers and the roar and clutter of the railway must have transformed the countryside for a few decades but all we see now are grassy humps and bumps in fields and a few derelict buildings.

There is still a lot to learn about Exmoor's historic environment so surveys are being made of the moor's archaeology and historic buildings. These will help us to understand how Exmoor has been used and lived on during the last 10,000 years and also help us to conserve our cultural heritage for future generations. Two special on-going projects are studies of 2000 years of iron-working on Exmoor and the history of the farmsteads on the moor.

HISTORIC SITES

More details of historic sites to visit can be found on page 56.

Brian Pearce

The Longstone, Challacombe

KEY DATES!

c 6800 BC First traces of human activity on Exmoor

c 4500 BC Neolithic people began to farm

c 2000 BC Bronze Age people built barrows and stone monuments

c 1000 BC Iron Age people built forts and hill-slope enclosures

c AD 43 The Romans built signal stations

AD 700-800 Saxons settled on Exmoor

11th–17th century Central Exmoor became a Royal Forest

1650 During the Civil War Exmoor Forest was sold to James Boevey

1818 Exmoor Forest was bought by John Knight

19th century Iron and copper mining

1897 The Knight estate sold to Lord Fortescue.

1954 Exmoor became a National Park.

1991 ENPA bought remaining moorland on the Exmoor part of the Fortescue Estate

1993 Exmoor became an ESA (Environmentally Sensitive Area)

1997 Exmoor National Park Authority became independent

THE WAY AHEAD LOOKS GOOD

Left: Eroded paths scar the landscape and damage surrounding habitats for wildlife.
Right: Care is taken to make sure that the work is of the highest standard and fits in with nearby landscape and habitat.

Exmoor National Park is a wonderful place to explore whether by foot, hoof or tyre. There are more than 1000km (625 miles) of public rights-of-way crossing the open heather moorland, farmland and wooded valleys, providing a varied choice of routes to suit everyone from the most intrepid hiker to the casual stroller. However, because Exmoor is so popular, paths are being eroded in some places.

From the mid-1990s organisations like the Exmoor National Park Authority, the National Trust and English Nature have been working together to improve the quality of access into the countryside and minimise the impact of wear on the landscape. Specially trained professional erosion staff have developed methods of improving the surface and the drainage of paths using local materials and resources.

This work, above and beyond the basic maintenance carried out by the National Park Authority, required additional funding and support. Many local businesses, especially those concerned with tourism, joined with the original partners to help generate support and funds for the work. Visitors, wanting to play their part in looking after Exmoor's unique habitats, were encouraged to make voluntary contributions wherever possible and many have done so.

Money has been raised for the work in all sorts of ways. Some visitors paid a levy on meals and bed nights in B&Bs, hotels and restaurants taking part in the scheme. Organisations giving the paths heavy usage made donations but one of the most unusual and perhaps most satisfying ways of raising funds and awareness was Purple Power! Heather seedlings were carefully taken from well-covered areas of moorland by National Trust volunteers. These were then propagated in a poly-tunnel. Once the plants had grown to a reasonable size, they were replanted along the edges of improved paths, speeding up the restoration of heather where it had been destroyed by trampling. Some plants were also sold in Selworthy and Dunster to raise money for equipping the volunteers with tools and clothing. This sustainable approach to conservation is definitely the way ahead and shared responsibility in a 'tourism and conservation partnership' for this, and similar projects, should keep Exmoor special for years to come.

THE ROYAL FOREST

The River Barle near Simonsbath with Exmoor Forest behind

16

The central area of Exmoor around Simonsbath is known as Exmoor Forest although there are very few trees. The word forest comes from the Latin *foras* meaning 'outside', in this case outside ordinary village law. When the Saxons moved onto Exmoor in the 700s they built their settlements below the spring line and left the exposed higher land with its poor soil to the wild animals. Saxon kings took responsibility for this area and under the Normans it became the property of the crown and a Royal Forest used mainly for hunting and grazing. There were strict laws designed to protect the wild red deer, enforced by officials who managed the Forest and prevented poaching and unauthorised use of the land.

Ponies, sheep and cattle were grazed on the moor and local tenants called 'suitors' provided the manpower to perambulate the boundaries and round up stock for checking. Apart from a short period during the Commonwealth when the Forest was sold to James Boevey, who built Simonsbath House, the Crown continued to own this area. Then, in 1818, it was sold to John Knight, a wealthy industrialist from Worcestershire. Knight had ambitious plans to develop an estate in the centre of Exmoor and the story of how he and his son, Frederic, introduced modern farming methods, built new farms and experimented with iron and copper mining can be read in *The Reclamation of Exmoor Forest*, by C.S. Orwin and *The Heritage of Exmoor* by Roger A. Burton (see page 64).

The ruins of Larkbarrow Farm

Brian Pearce

Today Exmoor Forest is a mixture of improved farmland and moorland, characterised by the grass *Molinia* commonly known as Purple Moor Grass or Flying Bent. It is aptly named for the grass is tinged with purple in the spring and then turns beige in winter when the brittle leaves are snapped by the frost and blown in the air to decorate the fences and hedgerows round about.

IDEAS FOR ENJOYING THE ROYAL FOREST

Explore Knight mining and farming country and visit the ruins of Wheal Eliza mine and the Iron Age earthwork of Cow Castle.
ENP Moorland Walk leaflet: Barle Valley, Simonsbath.

Walk out to Larkbarrow, a farm built by Frederic Knight. It was destroyed by army target practise during the Second World War. From Alderman's Barrow (SS 837 423) walk to Larkbarrow Gate and follow the marked track to Larkbarrow and Tom's Hill. Return via Kittuck (5 miles).

Explore Pinkworthy Pond and the Chains. The easiest route is from Goat Hill Bridge on the B3358 (SS 724 405) Simonsbath to Challacombe road. Walk up the track to Pinkworthy Pond, and across the boggy Chains to Chains Barrow. The path is signed but you will need a map. More information from ENP Visitor Centres.

Watch the skylarks circling overhead and listen to their trilling song

ENJOY THE VIEW!
There are great views from lay-bys near Five Barrows (SS 733 367) (views to Setta Barrow), Two Barrows (SS 747 362) (views over the Royal Forest and south over mid-Devon; and Prayway Head (SS 768 411) (view down Exe Valley). You'll find wonderful views across the moorland if you walk to Larkbarrow and Saddle Gate.

Visit one of the National Park Visitor Centres or Village Information Agencies for help with planning walk or cycle routes.

HEATHLAND

Hurlstone Point overlooking Porlock Vale

E. R. J. Davey

Perhaps the most spectacular scenery on Exmoor is the heathland which is almost blinding with its brilliant purples and gold. This is the moorland we truly associate with Exmoor and these areas were once the commons, used for grazing by farms and villages and surrounding Exmoor Forest. This heathland habitat is really rare, not just in this country but internationally.

The biggest areas of heathland can be found at Brendon, Withypool, on Dunkery Hill and at Wilmersham above Porlock. Most of this land is privately owned, some by the National Trust, but many public rights-of-way cross the commons and farmers are generous in granting more general access as long as the Country Code is observed.

This open heathland appears to be the most wild part of the moor but in fact its scenery is largely man-made and it is farmed. Heather, ling, gorse and bracken have replaced the sparse trees and bushes which once covered the tops of the Exmoor hills. Since prehistoric times people have cut down the trees and scrub to make fences and houses and for fuel, and grazing animals have prevented regrowth. Controlled burning has also been used to keep the growth down. Locally this burning is known as swaling and it takes place in early spring before the birds begin to build their nests. The idea is to clear the dead growth and allow fresh young shoots to appear which provide food for grazing but also, over the years, result in a patchwork of plants of different ages in different areas.

The best time to see the heathland is during the summer, especially when the ling is in full bloom. Ling is the plant that predominates and gives the moor its pinkish-purple colour. At this time of year you can hear and see bees buzzing all around in search of nectar. Some beekeepers put hives out on the edge of the heaths so that their bees will produce fragrant heather honey.

Especially beautiful at this time are the coastal heaths such as Holdstone Down, Countisbury Common, Yenworthy Common, Porlock Common, North Hill and Selworthy Beacon where bell heather with its deep purple flowers and the vivid yellow of western gorse bloom alongside ling. The southern heather moors including Anstey and Molland are quiet areas best enjoyed in early spring when morning mists swathe the countryside to the south and deer are often seen lying up in the undergrowth.

IDEAS FOR ENJOYING THE HEATHLAND

🚶 🚌 Walk in the Doone Country from County Gate (SS 794 487) or Malmsmead (SS 792 478). ENP Moorland Walk leaflet: Doone Country ($7^1/_2$ or 3 miles)

🚶 Walk on Haddon Hill from car park at Frogwell Lodge (SS 969 285). ENP Moorland Walk leaflet: Haddon Hill (6 or 3 miles)

🚶 Climb Dunkery Beacon, the highest spot on Exmoor at 1704 ft (519 m).

David Manners

'WARE ADDERS!

Many common lizards and adders live on the open moorland. The adder is Britain's only poisonous snake but it is rare for anyone to be bitten by one. It is very shy and will usually move into cover as people approach. However, when digesting a meal, especially in hot weather, the snake may be found sleeping in open areas including foot-paths. Not surprisingly a sleeping adder may resent being trodden on or poked with a stick and will react at once! So its worth taking care, with your dogs as well!

From the top there are extensive views across the Brendon Hills, the Bristol Channel and the heart of Exmoor. Approach via a minor road between Wheddon Cross and Luccombe. The shortest walk to the summit is from Dunkery Hill Gate ($^1/_2$ mile). On the same road between Kitbarrows and Robin How are laybys giving views down the Avill Valley to Dunster and the coast at Blue Anchor.

BE LIKE POOH BEAR!
Buy a jar or two of heather honey to take home as presents or to remind you of Exmoor during the long dark winter.

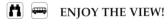 **ENJOY THE VIEW!**
There are wonderful views from the car parks on the A39 between Porlock and Lynmouth at Whitstones (top of Porlock Hill), County Gate and Barna Barrow (Countisbury). All are ideal starting points for exploring heathland on foot.

WATCH OUT FOR BIRDS OF PREY
Exmoor's wide open spaces are favourite hunting grounds for hawks and falcons The buzzard can often be spotted eyeing the ground from the top of a telegraph pole but it is unmistakable when it soars overhead on wings that measure more than a metre across. Kestrel and sparrow-hawk are also common but the hedgehopping flight of the hawk makes it less easy to identify than the soaring kestrel. There are a few pairs of merlin and peregrine falcon breeding on Exmoor but you'll be very lucky if you catch a glimpse of them!

How many different moths and butterflies can you spot? Grayling butterflies sit camouflaged on stony paths and the rare heath fritillary can be seen in some brackeny combes. Look out for caterpillars and beetles as well!

Photograph the gorse and heather or paint a picture in rich purple and gold.

Look out for Exmoor Ponies and Red Deer.

E.R.J. Davey

THE EXMOOR PONY

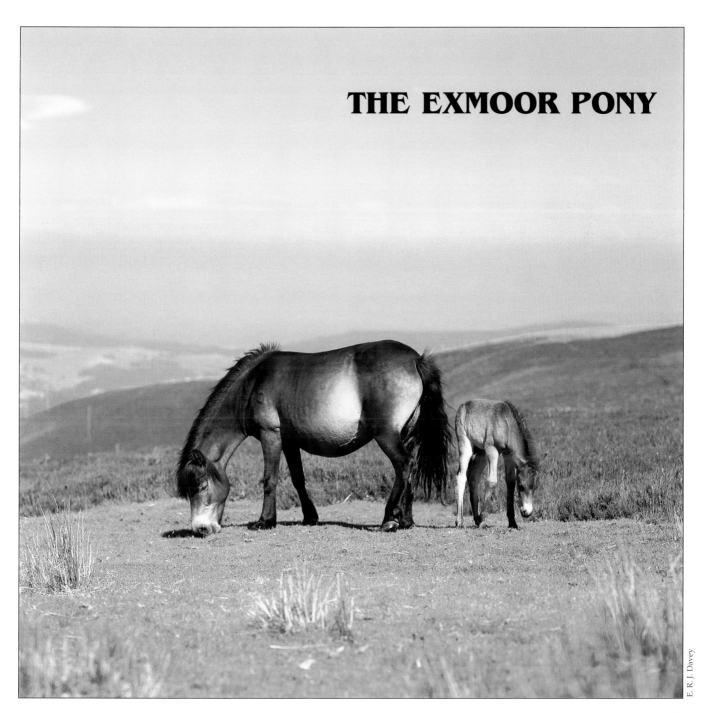

The Exmoor Pony is a very rare animal. There are just 1100 Exmoor Ponies in the world, far fewer than many recognised rare species like the Giant Panda. The pony has lived on Exmoor for longer than people have and is especially important because it is the nearest breed there is to the original wild horses of Europe. It has evolved in response to its environment, becoming hardy and resilient to the cold and wet.

These days the Exmoor Pony is only wild in the sense that the herds roam freely on the moor for all the ponies belong to somebody. A few years ago it was feared that the pony might become extinct so Exmoor National Park Authority bought young stock and now owns two herds. There are nine other privately owned herds.

The Exmoor Pony always breeds true to type. Its colouring ranges from dun (a smokey-brown) to bay (red-brown) or brown (dark brown). Its underparts and the area around the eyes and nose are a mealy buff colour while the mane, tail and points are black. The summer coat is fine and glossy but in the autumn the ponies grow a thick, two-layered protective coat. The true Exmoor is a sturdy pony, well-proportioned and sure footed. It has a large, well-shaped head with 'toad' eyes, large and dark, slightly hooded and set under a jutting brow which throws off the rain.

Foals are born in the spring and early summer and spend the summer running with their dams and building up a store of fat to take them through the hard winter ahead. When tourists are about, ponies tend to retreat to quiet areas of the moor where they can rest undisturbed. In the autumn the ponies are gathered from the moor and taken down to the farms; foals are weaned and all the ponies are inspected and branded before some are sold and the rest returned to the moor for the winter.

The Exmoor Pony Society was founded in 1921 to promote and encourage the breeding of pure-bred Exmoor Ponies. Contact: The Exmoor Pony Society, Glen Fern, Waddicombe, Dulverton TA22 9RY. 01398 341490

WHERE TO SEE EXMOOR PONIES

• Remember that the ponies are wild animals. Always approach ponies quietly and do nothing to disturb the herds. Do not on any account attempt to feed them,

• The two National Park herds run on Haddon Hill above Wimbleball Lake and on Warren, an open expanse of moorland between Exford and Simonsbath. Ponies can also be seen on Withypool Common, Winsford Hill, Dunkery Beacon, Lanacombe, Molland Moor and East and West Anstey Commons.

• Exford Show, held in August, is the Exmoor Pony Breed Show when ponies are shown in hand, under saddle and in harness.

• A comprehensive leaflet published by Exmoor National Park Authority and Exmoor Pony Society gives more information about the ponies and is available from ENP Visitor Centres or the Exmoor Pony Society.

THE WILD RED DEER

David Manners

Exmoor is famous for its Red Deer which have lived here since prehistoric times. There are large herds of Red Deer in Scotland but in England their numbers have decreased because, over the years, they have been killed for meat (venison) or because they damaged farmers' crops. There are now a few thousand in the Exmoor area, living on the open moor and using the woods and combes as places of safety.

Red Deer are the largest wild land animals in England. Adult males or stags stand 115 cm at the shoulder while females or hinds are about 15cm less. Only the stags grow horns or antlers and perhaps the most surprising fact is that they shed them and grow new ones each year. They are shed in April and early May and new ones start to grow immediately. The new growth is covered in a soft velvety skin which protects the spongy mass of sensitive blood vessels which hardens to form the horns. By about August the new 'head' is fully developed and the stag gets rid of the 'velvet' by rubbing its horns against a young tree. A young stag will produce only a couple of 'points' but as the stag gets older the new growth is longer and stronger until the full 'head' is developed when the stag is about ten. A healthy animal can live until it is about fifteen.

Except during the autumn rut or mating period, Red Deer normally form separate stag and hind herds, though you may occasionally see mixed herds or a single stag or hind and calf. They are mainly silent animals, but hinds will bark at intruders especially if their young are about or as a warning to the herd.

The rut or mating season begins early in the autumn. Stags start to gather up groups of hinds often with fierce arguments. The challenge roared out by a belligerent stag is known as belling or belving. This may be followed by the blood-curdling rattle of horns as two stags battle it out. Fights to the death are uncommon but the horns of a twenty-stone stag can prove a formidable weapon.

Calves are born in June and July and are usually dropped in moorland vegetation or by the edge of woodland. A single calf is normal and twins very rare. For a few days the calf will lie quietly, well camouflaged with dappled spots on its russet coat looking like sunlight on dead bracken. If you come across a calf do not touch it. Its mother will be nearby looking after it. Within a few days it will be able to nibble grass and in a couple of weeks is strong enough to run with its mother and join the herd. They stay together for a year or more.

E. R. J. Davey

Red Deer eat a wide variety of food, including young shoots of heather, whortle-berry, brambles, saplings and grass. They also feed on acorns, fungi, berries and ivy and can be a real pest to the farmer, raiding his fields for corn and root crops. They have eight biting teeth in front of the lower jaw but none immediately above, biting against a hard gum pad. Their footprints are called 'slots' and may often be found in the mud near a stream where deer come to drink. Their sight, hearing and sense of smell are excellent so it is quite difficult to get close to them.

FIND OUT MORE ABOUT RED DEER

Watch out for deer slots on muddy woodland paths and beside streams where the deer come to drink early in the morning and late in the evening.

Read the section on watching wildlife for some tips on spotting red deer.

Go for a walk with an expert. 'Deer searches' are organised by the ENP Rangers during the summer months. Details from ENP Visitor Centres. Private firms also organise similar excursions. Details in the Exmoor Visitor and the local press.

WOODLAND

E. R. J. Davey

Some of the most beautiful parts of Exmoor are wooded and this woodland is most important as a habitat for wildlife. At one time Exmoor was covered with broadleaf trees although many may have been little more than scruffy bushes or scrub. Once people began to farm on Exmoor these trees were cleared and now most of the earliest or 'ancient' woodland as it is known survives on steep valley sides and sea cliffs where ploughing is impossible and the land not much use for farming.

The old oak woodlands are particularly important and some form parts of areas designated as Sites of Special Scientific Interest. This designation is an indication of the quality and the variety of plants and animals to be found in the range of habitats in the woods. SSSIs include woods at Hawkcombe (just south of Porlock), along the Barle between Dulverton and Withypool, those between Watersmeet and Lynmouth and those in the Heddon Valley near Hunters Inn. Horner Wood is a National Nature Reserve. They are all worthwhile places to visit at any time of year.

Horner Wood, on the National Trust's Holnicote Estate, is an excellent example of how woods were once managed for agricultural and industrial purposes. At Cloutsham Ford there are ancient pollarded oak trees festooned with lichens, ferns and mosses. In the past they were topped at grazing height to produce a mass of green shoots for the benefit of stock grazing below. On the slopes can be seen scrub oak trees which were once coppiced – cut back on a short rotation to produce wood for making charcoal and tanbark for use in local tanneries. Other trees were grown as standards for timber – planks for ship-building and flooring, roof timbers and so on.

There are other old broadleaf woodlands in the Barle and Exe Valleys, along the coast at Woody Bay and between Glenthorne and Porlock. In these coastal areas the oaks were once coppiced and most trees are gnarled and stunted from the effects of exposure, lack of light and stony soil. Around Culbone the north-facing cliffs shade the trees from the sun, which is not seen at all during the winter. It's well worth walking the South West Coast Path which runs through these woods for a sense of peace and solitude.

More recently woods were planted in some areas for what is known these days as amenity; simply for people to enjoy. Sir Thomas Dyke Acland of Holnicote, the 10th Baronet, planted huge areas of woodland with mainly oak, evergreen oak and walnut on the hills behind Allerford and Bossington. It is said that a wood was planted on the occasion of the birth of each of his children. The evergreen holm oaks on Bossington Hill provide the area with a distinctly mysterious and Mediterranean atmosphere, especially on a hot summer's day. Victorian shrubs such as laurel and rhododendron which have been strangling the native trees are being cleared.

Around Dunster on the Luttrell estate, specially selected Douglas Fir seeds were planted in the 1860s and 1870s and these grew into the magnificent specimens to be seen along the road to Broadwood Farm. A Douglas Fir here features in the *Guinness Book of Records* for 1993 as the tallest tree in England. The track running between them towards the farm is known as Cathedral Walk because it is like walking along the pillared aisles of a cathedral.

Modern conifer plantations, grown as crops and always changing, can also be attractive especially when combined with good views. The main plantations are just south of Dunster on the Brendon Hills. Here there are plenty of wide rides used as footpaths and cycle tracks as well as picnic sites and some play areas for children. Surprisingly these woods remain some of the quietest parts of the National Park and are especially enjoyed by local people.

Woodland owned by Exmoor National Park Authority includes an unusual beech wood, Birch Cleave at Simonsbath, and old oak woods at Hawkcombe (Porlock), Culbone, Dulverton and Timberscombe. When old woods are no longer being managed in traditional ways they may become dark and overgrown, and non-native trees that are poorer for wildlife, like the sycamore and the sweet chestnut, spread. In order to conserve the landscape and the wildlife the ENPA are thinning out old oak coppice, felling conifers and non-native trees and, in places, re-coppicing and re-pollarding. This lets in the light, gives the trees a chance to regenerate and allows glades and rides to be opened up. It also provides a better habitat for creatures like the rare fritillary butterflies and the wood ant.

Farmers and other landowners are being encouraged to manage their woodlands more positively for conservation which will help job creation in woodland management and promote the manufacture of woodland products which range from charcoal for the barbecue to quality bespoke furniture. These can all be bought locally.

E. R. J. Davey

Clockwise from top left: Wood ants' nest, Wood mouse, Jonquils, Ferns at the water's edge

WOODLAND WILDLIFE

Woodland provides rich habitats for all sorts and sizes of wildlife. They are home, for example, to the wild Red Deer and to wood mice and the much rarer dormouse. Look out for hazel nut shells with the distinctive round hole gnawed by the dormouse.

When branches and even whole trees come down in a storm they are frequently left to provide a home for a wide variety of insects, mosses and fungi. The seething heaps of tiny twigs that you often find in woodland are the nests of the wood ant, much larger than its garden cousin. If you look carefully you will see hundreds of ants all purposefully running hither and thither each carrying a burden.

Plants in woodland include some of the earliest spring flowers. Before January is over, a few primroses are out in sheltered corners to confirm its reputation as the 'first rose' of the new season. Celandines also appear in January, their shiny yellow petals cheering the dreary winter days. They are soon joined by carpets of wild snowdrops in woods near Wheddon Cross and in hedgerows on the Brendons. Soon to follow are wood sorrel, wild daffodils or jonquils near Sully, wood anemones at Treborough and in the woods by Wimbleball Lake, and masses of bluebells in the Barle and Exe valleys. Other common woodland plants include the tiny moschatel, wood sanicle, enchanters nightshade, cow-wheat, wood speedwell and yellow pimpernel.

Ferns grow best in moist woods, the most abundant on Exmoor being lady and male ferns, shield fern, hard fern, hart's tongue, polypody and the lemon scented or mountain fern. Rare species still to be found include oak, beech, and hay scented ferns and grassland species. An 1811 directory for Porlock refers to a 'fern-gatherer' who sent his wares up to London. Nowadays we don't expect to pick flowers or ferns but leave them for other people to enjoy.

In many of the broadleaf woods mosses and lichens adorn the trees, some hanging from the branches like lacy green curtains and others colouring trunk and branches with textured grey, green and yellow. The presence of lichens denotes a pollution-free zone so Horner Wood with over 100 species, many very rare, must have some of the cleanest air in England!

Walking in the woods one may be startled by a buzzard swooping below the branches to reach its nest. The old oak woodlands are home to a multitude of birds offering not only holes and branches for nesting but also insects and berries for food. Green, great spotted and lesser spotted woodpeckers are regular inhabitants as well as nuthatches and tree-creepers. Beside tits, chaffinches, robins, jays, thrushes and blackbirds, summer visitors include wood and willow warblers, chiffchaffs, spotted flycatchers, blackcaps, redstarts and pied flycatchers.

IDEAS FOR ENJOYING WOODLAND

Walk in Horner Wood or in the woods above Selworthy and Bossington. NT walk leaflets are available from NT shops and ENP Visitor Centres.

Walk beside the river Barle through Birch Cleave, farmland and conifer plantations. ENP Moorland Walk leaflet: Barle Valley, Simonsbath. (9 miles)

Climb a hundred steps through woodland on the National Trust Centenary walk. Wonderful views at the top. Start SS 889 464

ENJOY THE VIEW! You will need to walk to reach the best viewpoints over woodland though there are good views from roads at Webber's Post and Ley Hill (over Horner Woods) and at Langham Hill (over Chargot Wood to Croydon Hill). Well worth the walk are these viewpoints: Sugarloaf Hill (overlooking Glenthorne Pinetum and coastal woods) reached from A39 at County Gate; Wind Hill (overlooking Watersmeet) from Countisbury; Myrtleberry Cleave (also overlooking Watersmeet) from Lynmouth or

Hillsford Bridge; Gallox Hill (overlooking Croydon Hill and Broadwood) from Dunster via Deer Park; Haddon Hill and Wimbleball Dam (overlooking Haddeo Valley) from B3190 at Frogwell Lodge.

Bike it through Dunster Woods. There are three trails at family, intermediate and explorer levels, all starting from Nutcombe Bottom near Dunster. Leaflet available from ENP Visitor Centres.

Take the children to Nutcombe Bottom near Dunster to enjoy the Crown Estate play and picnic area set in woodland and to find the tallest tree in England nearby. There are some good way-marked walks from here. Leaflet available.

Look at the lichens in Horner Wood! See how many different sorts you can spot on one tree, but don't touch!

Find a fallen tree and count how many different creepy-crawlies you can see in it.

Sit quietly and listen the sounds of the woodland. Write a poem.

Capture a gnarled tree or the subtle colours of new growth, mosses and lichens in a painting or photograph.

E. R. J. Davey

FRESHWATER

Hoar Oak Water

David Manners

31

There are many beautiful rivers on Exmoor, the largest being the Exe and the Barle. Both are renowned for their fishing but it is easier to get to the Barle which makes it more popular with visitors. The river runs right beside the Exmoor National Park Authority offices at Dulverton and many people enjoy sitting quietly, picnicking beside the river here. Dulverton's Barle Bridge has been enlarged to accommodate modern traffic, but some twelve miles upstream at Landacre is a perfectly preserved medieval bridge. Landacre is popular as a picnic site beside the river and open moorland of Withypool Common.

About three miles below Landacre is the arched bridge at Withypool and youngsters enjoy swimming in the river here. A few miles to the south, Lower Willingford Bridge over Dane's Brook, a tributary of the Barle, is an attractive and quiet picnic spot. Winsford is one of the most popular spots on the River Exe with seven bridges over the river and Winn Brook. Nearby on the Barle is Tarr Steps, a clapper bridge and one of the most popular beauty spots within Exmoor National Park. It's definitely a place to be avoided during the day in the busy summer.

Packhorse bridges were built so that pack ponies could transport their loads of wool and other goods when river levels were high. Some are medieval and others more modern. These picturesque bridges include those at Allerford and Horner and Gallox Bridge at Dunster.

Waterfalls are another great attraction and these are common on the rapid northward-flowing streams near and on the coast. Many of the little streams which tumble down the cliffs end abruptly in vertical falls. Most are difficult to reach and are best seen from the sea. The falls at Woody Bay and Glenthorne are worth the steep walk. Most popular, however, are the falls on Hoaroak Water between Watersmeet and Hillsford Bridge, on the East Lyn between Watersmeet and Lynmouth and the West Lyn Gorge at Lynmouth (where there is an entrance fee).

Above: Bullhead or miller's thumb
Below: Grey Wagtail

There are four reservoirs in or near the National Park at Wimbleball, Nutscale, Wistland-pound and Clatworthy. Wimbleball is by far the largest and provides facilities for walking, picnicking, nature study, sailing, fishing and camping. It's an excellent place to take the children; refreshments are available in the summer months and there's plenty of space to run about and explore.

Fast flowing rivers and streams provide ideal conditions for many birds including the grey wagtail, heron and mallard with the little white-breasted dipper a familiar sight bobbing up and down on a mid-stream boulder. Occasionally a flash of brilliant blue will announce the presence of the king-fisher. The coot, tufted duck, pochard and little grebe are winter visitors to the reservoirs where Canada geese can often be seen. In the rivers you may see small trout and occasionally a small salmon jumping and in slower streams there are minnows, stickleback, stone loach and the eel-like brook lamprey with its strange sucker around the mouth. Exmoor's beautiful dragonflies and damselflies often surprise and delight.

David Manners

David Manners

IDEAS FOR ENJOYING RIVERS, STREAMS AND RESERVOIRS

Lift a stone on a stream bed to see what lives underneath. (Put the stone back where you found it!)

Paddle at East Water, Cloutsham.

Walk beside the Barle between Dulverton, Tarr Steps and Withypool. ENP Country Walks leaflets: Barle Valley, Dulverton; Dulverton to Brushford. Also bus timetable walks.

Enjoy a picnic beside a river. Popular sites are at Robbers' Bridge, East Water, Cloutsham and near Landacre Bridge.

Shut your eyes and listen to the water. Write a poem.

Walk or bike it around Wimbleball Lake. Leaflets available.

Try your hand at fishing (see page 50). You will need a licence and maybe a permit.

Draw or paint a picture of a bridge. There are picturesque bridges at Allerford, Horner and Withypool.

Enjoy a cream tea at Horner or Watersmeet.

Visit Lynmouth and discover what happened when the town was flooded in 1952.

Packhorse bridge at Brendon

E. R. J. Davey

Exmoor's coastline is magnificent and in 1991 it was designated a Heritage Coast. The cliffs are the highest in England. The headlands facing west receive a battering from the Atlantic gales and have vertical cliff faces as high as 390m (1280ft) on Great Hangman but those facing north are sheltered from the predominant south-westerly winds and here the rounded 'hog's back' reflects the shape of the Exmoor hills and slope more gently towards the sea.

The stretch of coast between Porlock Weir and Woody Bay is heavily wooded and twisted and stunted oak trees grow right down to the beach some even growing among the beach pebbles above the tide line. Here there's an unusual mixture of woodland and sea birds, woodpeckers and jays mixing with fulmars and oyster-catchers. Occasionally a Red Deer ventures to the beach, Once these woods would have resounded to the sound of metal on wood as the trees were coppiced or felled. Later landowners built carriage drives so that they might enjoy the views in comfort.

The most dramatic part of the coastline is the section between the Valley of Rocks and Heddon's Mouth and here in early summer you can see guillemots and razor-bills flying to and from their nests to feed their young

Castle Rock and Duty Point

Brian Pearce

E. R. J. Davey

The lighthouse at Countisbury

while the calls of jackdaw, fulmar, kittiwake and raven mingle above. It is on Holdstone Down and Great Hangman, as on Bossington Hill, that one can obtain the special feeling of Exmoor for this is where the heathland meets the sea and the scent of gorse mingles with the salty sea breezes.

TIDE CHECK!

If you're going on the beach check the tides! Tide time-tables are available from newsagents and fishing tackle shops at Minehead, Lynmouth and Combe Martin, from ENP Visitor Centres and are published weekly in the *West Somerset Free Press* and the *North Devon Journal*.

IDEAS FOR ENJOYING THE COAST

🚶 Walk a part of the South West Coast Path. This path begins at Minehead and runs for 600 miles (966km) around the south-west peninsula to Studland Bay in Dorset. The ENPA publishes a guide to the section of the path between Minehead and Combe Martin. It breaks the walk into sections with alternative return routes which form long and short circular walks. Full details from ENP Visitor Centres. N.B. At Porlock Bay the Coast Path has been diverted because of damage to the shingle ridge. If you walk along Bossington beach, take special care.

🚶 Look out for the White Lady, the Devil's Cheesewring and Rugged Jack in the Valley of Rocks; ENP Country Walk leaflet: Valley of Rocks. Start Bottom Meadow car park, Castle Hill, Lynton (SS 721 493).

🔭 **VIEW THE COAST FROM THE SEA!**
Enquire at Lynmouth and Combe Martin ENP Visitor Centres for details of boat trips with a guide.

🚶 There are paths down to the beach at Wild Pear Beach (Combe Martin), Lee Bay, and Wringcliff Bay, (Lynton). Remember there's always a steep climb back!

🚶 🚌 Take a guided walk on the Hangman Hills near Combe Martin. Details from ENP Visitor Centres and in the *Exmoor Visitor*.

🚶 **TO THE LIGHTHOUSE!**
Walk out to the lighthouse at Countisbury above Lynmouth. Start at Barna Barrow car park SS 753 497

🚗 If you need to use a car drive the scenic route along North Hill, Minehead. There are wonderful views over Porlock Bay to Foreland Point from the Bossington Hill car park.

⛵ Visit one of the harbour villages; Porlock Weir, Lynmouth or Combe Martin. Look out for fresh fish to buy for your evening meal.

🧭 Visit Ilfracombe or Minehead for that seaside town experience

📖 Read *The Overland Launch* by C. Walter Hodges, the exciting story of how the Lynmouth lifeboat was taken overland to be launched at Porlock Weir. Available from ENP Visitor Centres or by mail/credit card. Tel. 01398 323665

FARMLAND

David Manners

Much of Exmoor is a patchwork quilt of farmsteads, fields of grass and crops, stitched together by high hedgebanks and stone walls. Framed by valley, woodland and hill-top heathland, it is an essential and well-loved part of the Exmoor scene.

There is little arable farming on Exmoor save in low-lying areas like the Vale of Porlock, around Combe Martin, and along the northern edge of the Brendons between Withycombe and Monksilver. At Combe Martin there is mainly market gardening, particularly strawberry growing on the south facing slopes of the Umber Valley. Here you can see a multitude of narrow strip-shaped fields formed by the enclosure of medieval open fields. In the Vale of Porlock and on the Brendon Hills it is corn-growing country, traditionally for fine malting barley. On the hillsides are lynchets – terraces where crops have been grown since medieval times or earlier. Occasionally you can see a field where the wheat stands in stooks, ready to be used for traditional thatching.

David Manners

John Richards hedge-laying at Ash Farm near Porlock.

On the high plateau it is the beech hedges which dominate. Largely a part of late nineteenth and early twentieth century enclosure of moorland, it is hard to imagine Exmoor without them. In the past hedges were laid by hand but today are usually cut mechanically though you can still see the traditional craft of hedge-laying being practised.

Around Simonsbath, the centre of the nineteenth century reclamation of Exmoor, there are dry stone walls reminiscent of northern England and Scotland. Many were made by shepherds from these areas tempted to Exmoor by the Knight family. In the fields can be seen local hardy breeds; Devon Red Ruby cattle and Exmoor Horn and Devon Closewool sheep.

Primroses

Many wild animals move between moor, woodland and farmland often making use of the areas where different types of land meet. There are plenty of rabbits, wood mice, bank and short-tailed voles but fewer brown hares. Stoats and weasels prey on the smaller mammals living on the margins of moorland and in hedgebanks. The fox, too, is common and you might come across a fox's earth almost anywhere within the National Park. The badger which also has its home underground is increasing in numbers and the earthy mouths of their setts are common. Badgers are nocturnal and, like hedgehogs, are often killed on the road during the night.

A vast number of colourful flowers and other plants live happily together in the hedgerows and narrow lanes of Exmoor. Early ones include ground ivy, dog's mercury, primrose, daisy – the day's eye – and dandelion, named from the French dent-de-lion meaning lion's tooth. You will see why if you examine the next dandelion leaf you come across. By May there is cow parsley, pink-flowered herb Robert, red campion, buttercups, sweet violets and Jack-by-the-hedge, sometimes called 'sauce alone' and once valued in the springtime for its oniony flavour. There are masses of foxgloves and later rose bay willow herb.

On drier banks there is sure to be bird's-foot trefoil, sheep's bit scabious, woodsage, mallow, English stonecrop, and wall pennywort, common enough on Exmoor but missing from most of England. Shining cranesbill with gleaming green leaves and pink flowers is another fairly common plant here but enthused about by visiting botanists. Among the last to flower are blue field scabious, yellow toadflax, autumn lady's tresses orchid and pink centaury. The seventeenth century herbalist, Nicholas Culpeper wrote that centaury is 'very wholesome but not very toothsome but virtuous for removing freckles.' Hedgerow birds include the yellow bunting or yellow-hammer with its distinctive song, 'little bit of bread and no cheese', the dunnock, or hedge sparrow, green finch and bull finch.

E. R. J. Davey

IDEAS FOR ENJOYING FARMLAND

Many Exmoor footpaths cross farmland and it is important to remember that the land is the farmer's working environment. Remember to close gates and keep dogs on leads as you go through fields.

Farm walks. Details of farmers providing farm walks can be obtained from ENP Visitor Centres.

SETTLEMENTS

E. R. J. Davey

Exmoor's towns and villages are as attractive, interesting and varied as her habitats. About 10,500 people live on Exmoor, half in the villages and the rest in tiny hamlets and scattered farms and cottages. The only settlements in the National Park that are large enough to be called towns are Dulverton, Lynton and Lynmouth and Porlock. Most settlements have never grown to be more than a few farmhouses and cottages with maybe a shop. Dunster is an exception. It prospered in medieval times around its castle and market and today is one of the best preserved English medieval villages. The coastal settle-ments, Lynmouth, Combe Martin and Porlock Weir all developed initially as fishing harbours and ports for trade in the Bristol Channel and elsewhere. Thatched fishermen's cottages and old lime kilns reflect this past. At Porlock Weir some of the cottages with strange names like Gibralter and Turkey seem to have the beach as their back gardens. Lynton and Lynmouth were linked origi-nally by a steep cliff path. The installation of the famous water-powered cliff railway followed their development as holiday resorts in the nineteenth century. Guide books of the time compared the area to Switzerland and

Brian Pearce

Lynmouth – the harbour and Mars Hill.

41

many of the hotels and guest houses were built in Swiss chalet style, with carved gable ends and balconies facing the sea.

Some of the most attractive settlements are villages and hamlets in the Vale of Porlock. Selworthy with its lime-washed church, a landmark for miles around, is one of the most popular. The pretty Green is surrounded by thatched cottages re-modelled from farm houses in the 1820s for retired workers on the Holnicote estate which then belonged to the Acland family, now to the National Trust.

Local cottages are usually plain and simple, built on a rectangular plan which has developed from the ancient longhouse pattern. Small casement windows and arched doorways are traditional while larger cottages some-times have an elaborate porch with a room built over it. Tall chimneys are a local feature especially when placed on the front wall of the cottage. They have often been extended upwards to improve the draw of the fire and frequently have an extension at the bottom where bread ovens were built at the back of the large open fireplace inside.

Building stone in the Exmoor region is poor and cannot be cut neatly. As a result many cottages were built of rubble or even of cob – a mixture of mud, straw, dung and stone. Most are limewashed to keep the rain from the porous stone. The traditional pink colour wash is said to have been made by mixing pig's blood with whitewash.

Other cottages and farmhouses have slates hung on their windward walls to keep out the rain. The poor building materials lend themselves to rounded shapes for corners, chimneys and pillars and add to the cosy appearance of the cottages. Roofing material is traditionally wheat straw, although this is frequently replaced with slate. On the Devon side the slate is often original. Typical unspoilt Exmoor settlements include Stoke Pero, Trentishoe, Twitchen, Hawkridge, Withiel Florey and Treborough.

There are few large mansions in the area for Exmoor was never a region of rich estates. Examples include Dunster Castle, of Norman foundation and rebuilt in Tudor and Victorian times; Nettlecombe Court, now a field studies centre; Combe Sydenham near Monksilver, linked with Francis Drake; Doverhay Manor in Porlock, which now houses the museum; and Pixton Park at Dulverton, home of the Herbert family.

Most Exmoor churches were established in the twelfth century although all contain alterations and additions. The ruins of the Cistercian Cleeve Abbey at Washford are magnificent but just a few stones are left of St Nicholas Priory at Barlynch near Dulverton (private). Perhaps the finest religious building is the parish church of St George at Dunster which was built to serve the needs of both Benedictine monks and parishioners. Wealth from wool contributed to its glories. In contrast Exmoor boasts some of the smallest churches in England in regular use; at Culbone deep in the woods west of Porlock Weir, at Stoke Pero high on the moor south of Porlock village and at Trentishoe.

Interesting dissenting chapels on Exmoor include the Congregational Chapel at Dulverton and Beulah Chapel near Raleigh's Cross. The latter was built to serve the mining community centred on the iron mines worked on the Brendons during the last century.

GAZETTEER

SELECTED TOWNS AND VILLAGES OF EXMOOR

Allerford SS 905 470 Shop and PO CP PC Museum VIA
Domesday hamlet in the parish of Selworthy, now largely NT, with a picturesque medieval packhorse bridge.

Barbrook SS 715 477 Petrol Shop PO VIA
Hamlet on West Lyn severely damaged in 1952 flood but bridge rebuilt.

Bossington SS 898 478 CP PC
Ancient hamlet which in Saxon times belonged to the Abbot of Athelney. Now largely NT. Lies between Allerford and the sea. Good starting place for walks. Early 16th century Lynch Chapel was restored in 1885 after being used as a barn.

Brendon SS 769 482 Shop Inns
Small village set in the beautiful wooded valley of the East Lyn just on the Devon border. Name means 'broom hill', no

Bossington

connection with the Brendons (brown hills). Parish church dedicated to St Brendan, Celtic missionary to Devon, nearly two miles from village. Good centre for fishing, riding and walking.

Bridgetown SS 923 332 Shop Inn
ENP Country Walk leaflet: Winsford and Bridgetown
Hamlet by the river Exe in Exton parish. On A396 midway between Wheddon Cross and Dulverton. Pleasant riverside cricket ground.

Brompton Regis SS 954 314 Shop Inn VIA
Quiet village with many scattered farms in the Brendon Hills and an interesting church.

Brushford SS 920 258 Inn
ENP Country Walk leaflet: Dulverton to Brushford
Small village near River Barle, two miles south of Dulverton. Pixton Park nearby was home of the Herbert family. Ancient oak in churchyard and chapel designed by Lutyens (1926).

Bury SS 945 275
Small, delightful village, some thatch, in Haddeo valley, Brendon foothills, on by-road two miles east of Dulverton. Ford through river and beautiful, very narrow packhorse bridge. Strongly advised not to attempt either by car but very photogenic. Bury Castle nearby, remains of Norman motte-and-bailey.

Carhampton ST 009 425 Shop PO Inn
Pronounced C'rampton. Large busy village on A39 three miles east of Minehead with impressive church and painted screen. It once belonged to King Alfred and has legends of King Arthur, St Carantoc and the dragons (Viking ships) which ravaged this coast a thousand years ago. The custom of apple wassailing on 17 January (Old Twelfth Night) is still carried on.

Challacombe SS 694 410 PO Inn VIA
Moorland village two miles inside Devon on B3358. The name

means 'cold valley' and the local inn has the interesting name, the Black Venus.

Clatworthy ST 052 308
Small village in the Brendon Hills. Reservoir formed by damming the River Tone in 1961 is a peaceful setting for fishing and walks, including nature trail.

Combe Martin SS 585 465 CP PC Inns Refreshments Shops PO ENP Visitor Centre Museum
ENP Village Walk leaflet: Combe Martin
Named after Martin de Tours, a friend of William the Conqueror. Long straggling village 1^1/$_2$ miles long along the Umber valley. SW side quarried for limestone, ochre and umber while NE side mined for lead, silver and iron. Market gardening and tourism.

Countisbury SS 747 498 Inn
Coastal hamlet at top of famous hill with church and 16th century inn, once the Blue Ball, now the Sandpiper Inn.

Cutcombe SS 930 392
See Wheddon Cross

Dulverton SS 915 280 CP Petrol PC Inns Refreshments Shops PO ENP Visitor Centre
ENP Village Walk leaflet: Dulverton   ENP Country Walk leaflet: Dulverton to Brushford

Dulverton from Andrews Hill

Quiet little town of narrow streets with medieval bridge over the River Barle. Exmoor House, originally the Union Workhouse, is now the offices of the National Park Authority. Guildhall Centre houses museum, art gallery and the Exmoor Photographic Archive.

Dunster SS 990 437 CP (very limited parking in village) PC Inns Refreshments Shops ENP Visitor Centre
ENP Village Walk leaflet: Dunster
ENP Country Walks leaflet: Grabbist and Gallox Hill
One of Exmoor's most attractive and popular villages. It prospered in medieval times through the trade of wool and woollen cloth and today is one of England's best preserved examples of a medieval village despite the modern traffic. Fine medieval buildings include the castle, priory church, tithe barn, dovecote, working mill, packhorse bridge, and Luttrell Arms Hotel, once the residence of the Abbots of Cleeve. The famous Yarn Market dates from the early 17th century. Dunster Castle is in the care of the National Trust (01643 821318) and is open from April to October as is the restored watermill. The castle gardens are open every day save Christmas Day. There are plenty of places for refreshment and shops of all kinds including crafts, gifts, leather, paintings and clothes. Somerest Guild of Craftsmen's Gallery is open all the year round. Dunster Dolls Museum houses more than 700 dolls.

East Anstey SS 867 265 Inn
Village just south of National Park boundary with church of St Michael and Froude Arms Inn.

Elworthy ST 083 350
Tiny village on B3188 Watchet to Wiveliscombe road.

Exford SS 855 384 CP Petrol PC Inns Refreshments Shops
ENP Village Walk leaflet: Exford
On River Exe in the heart of the National Park. Busy hunting, fishing and walking centre. Hotels, guest houses and youth hostel.

Exton SS 926 337 (PO, shop and inn at Bridgetown).
Old Domesday settlement. The church and few houses are set on the side of the hill east of the A396.

Hawkridge SS 862306
Lonely village set high above the Dane's Brook and River Barle.

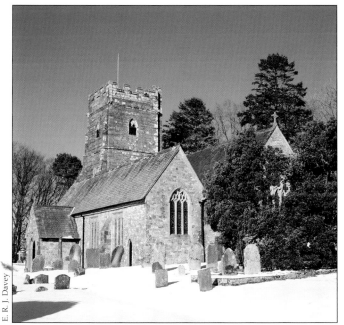

Exford church in winter

Best reached from Dulverton. The church of St Giles has a Norman doorway and white-washed interior. Keeps up old tradition of 'revel' in form of summer gymkhana.

High Bray SS 691 344
Interesting settlement with All Saints' Church commanding the summit of a small hill overlooking the Bray valley and Brayford below.

Kentisbury SS 622 439
Scattered settlement straddling the National Park boundary. The church of St Thomas has a fine 15th century tower.

Leighland ST 033 365
Isolated hamlet in Brendon Hills between Roadwater and Raleigh's Cross. The church once belonged to Cleeve Abbey and was restored in 1862.

Luccombe SS 910 445
Picturesque village, formerly part of the Acland estate, is mostly owned by National Trust. Beautifully set among trees at the foot of Robin How. Traces of iron ore mining.

Luxborough SS 974 380 Inn
Village divided into three, Kingsbridge, Pooltown and Churchtown, in valley between Brendon and Croydon Hills. Remnants of iron mining. Church has unusual saddleback tower.

Lynmouth SS 725 495 CP PC Shops Inns Refreshments ENP Visitor Centre
ENP Village Walk leaflet: Lynmouth
The village built alongside river and sea is justly famous for its picturesque setting and developed initially as fishing harbour and port for coastal trade. Thatched fishermen's cottages; kilns for burning lime. Largely rebuilt after disastrous flood of 1952. Cliff railway connects with Lynton.

Lynton SS 720 495 CP Shops PO Inns Refreshments PC Museum Information Centre.
ENP Village Walk leaflet: Lynton
ENP Country Walks leaflet: Watersmeet, Valley of Rocks
Popular small holiday resort developed in 19th century. Spectacular cliff walk to the Valley of Rocks.

Martinhoe SS 668 487
Small village set among hills near the Devon border.

Molland SS 808 284 Inns
Lies just south of the National Park above Yeo valley. The 15th century church has a well preserved 18th century interior with box pews and three-decker pulpit.

Monksilver ST 073 374 Inn
Rural village in attractive valley on B3188. Silver comes from the Latin *silva* meaning woodland. A mile away is Combe Sydenham, a 16th century house which was the home of Elizabeth Sydenham, second wife of Sir Franis Drake.

Nettlecombe ST 056 378
Scattered settlement near the B3188. The church is full of interest while the 16th century Court, long the home of the Trevelyans, is now a field study centre.

North Molton SS 736 299 CP Inn Shops
Once a prosperous small town due to wool and then to copper and iron mining. It is now a peaceful place. The fine parish church has a large tower and interesting interior. The nearby Court House is the historic home of the Bampfylde family.

Oare SS 802 473 (CP PC Refreshments and Shop [summer] at nearby Malmsmead)
Famous for its church which was the setting of the marriage between Jan Ridd and Lorna Doone in R.D. Blackmore's novel.

Old Cleeve ST 041 419 (Inns and PO at Washford)
One of the largest Exmoor parishes including the villages of Old Cleeve, Washford and Roadwater.

Parracombe SS 670 450 Inn PC Shop PO VIA
ENP Country Walk leaflet: Parracombe
Built below the modern A39 road between Lynton and Barnstaple in the valley of the River Heddon. The ancient church of St Petrock with its interesting Georgian interior has been preserved although replaced in Victorian times by a church nearer the centre of the village. From the new church can be seen the remains of the Norman motte and bailey Holwell Castle.

Porlock SS 885468 CP Petrol PC Inns Refreshments Shops PO Museum Information Centre
ENP Village Walk leaflet: Porlock ENP Country Walk: Porlock Bay
Busy village at foot of notorious Porlock Hill surrounded by hills save on the seaward side. There is an attractive combination of thatched cob cottages and Victorian buildings in Porlock. Porlock Weir is a mile and a half down the road beside the sea. St Dubricius church and Porlock museum are of interest.

Porlock Weir SS 865 478 CP PC Inns Refreshments Shops
ENP Country Walk: Porlock Bay
Sheltered by Worthy Woods, it looks across Porlock Bay to Hurlstone Point. The tiny harbour with lock gates was once busy with coastal trade. Now it is mainly used by pleasure craft.

Roadwater ST 032 382 Inn Shop PO
Long straggling village in Old Cleeve parish. Good starting point for walks.

Rodhuish ST 017 396
Straggling hamlet in parish of Withycombe and a Domesday manor. Its name means dwelling-place of the radman or judge. Tiny church of St Bartholomew boasts a west gallery.

J.D. Anderson

Selworthy

Selworthy SS 920 468 CP PC Refreshments NT Shop and information centre.
Picturesque village of ornate thatched cottages. Those around the Green were altered to house former servants of the Aclands who once owned the Holnicote estate, now National Trust. Fine medieval church with extensive views across the Vale of Porlock towards Dunkery.

Simonsbath SS 775 394 CP Refreshments Inn
Pronounced Simmonsbath. Thought to mark the place where Sigmund's path crossed the River Barle. Centre of the Knight empire in the 19th century. Good starting-point for walks.

Skilgate SS 987 272
Small village in the Brendon Hills. Church of St John largely restored in the 19th century.

Stoke Pero SS 878 435
Scattered village of nine farms. The small church at 309m (1014ft) is one of the highest on Exmoor. Its date and dedication are lost but the list of incumbents begins in 1242 with John: parson of Stoke. Pero comes from the name of the family who held land here about 1300.

Timberscombe SS 956 420 Inn PO
Just off the A396, the Saxon name of this small village means 'wooded valley'.

Treborough ST 010 364
Consists of a small, plain church and a few buildings exposed over 304m (998ft) up on the northern side of the Brendon Hills. Name means 'place of waterfall'. Once had important slate quarries.

Trentishoe SS 646 486
Tiny village not far from mouth of the River Heddon. The small church still has its musician's gallery.

Twitchen SS 790 305
On Exmoor's southern slopes, this village consists of farms and a few houses clustered round the church of St Peter.

Upton SS 994 290 Petrol Inn
Small village along the B3190 on the eastern edge of Haddon Hill. Ruined tower and foundations of old church lie a mile away near Upton Farm.

West Anstey SS 852 275
The small and ancient church of St Petrock has a fine Norman font. On West Anstey Common nearby is a memorial erected in 1935 to Philip Froude Hancock, a celebrated local huntsman.

Winsford SS 905 350 Petrol Inn Shop PO VIA
ENP Country Walk leaflet: Winsford and Bridgetown
Attractive village with at least seven bridges set in wide valley amid wooded hills; best reached by turning off the A396. Birthplace of Labour politician, Ernest Bevin.

Withiel Florey SS 987 334
Parish of scattered farms and 15th century church amid the green fields of the Brendon Hills.

Wheddon Cross SS 925 388 Petrol PC Inn Shops PO VIA
Highest point on the A396 between Exmoor and the Brendon Hills. In parish of Cutcombe. Cattle market.

Winsford

Withycombe ST 015 413
Village of old picturesque cottages and interesting church off the A39. Named from the withies or willows that still grow by the village stream.

Withypool SS 845 356 Petrol PC Inn Shop PO VIA
Ancient village on the River Barle. Handsome five-arched bridge and church dedicated to St Andrew. Writer on Somerset life, Walter Raymond, lived here from 1905 to 1914 and R.D. Blackmore wrote part of Lorna Doone while staying at the Royal Oak Inn.

Wootton Courtenay ST 938 434 Petrol Inn Shop PO VIA
Village stretching for more than a mile along the lower slopes of Wootton Common. Wonderful carved bosses in the roof of All Saints' church.

WHAT TO DO ON EXMOOR

WALKING

While riding may be the traditional way of getting about on Exmoor, walking is definitely the most popular activity and definitely the best way of seeing the moor. Exmoor can offer the walker something for all tastes and abilities from a quiet evening stroll to a twenty mile trek. There are over 1000km (625m) of public footpaths and bridlepaths with countryside rugged enough to challenge the most experienced rambler and beautiful enough to tempt the laziest couch potato!

Exmoor National Park Authority does a great deal to help the walker. Rights-of-way are maintained, paths are signed with finger posts and often waymarked with coloured squares and arrows. This helps those who are not too good at map-reading

Near Badgworthy water

to find their way and avoid private property. Many of these walks are described in detail in easy-to-understand, colourful leaflets which can be obtained at ENP Visitor Centres where staff will give advice and help you make sure of the route. Most of the walks suggested in this book are based on leaflet walks which provide a map and detailed instructions together with background information. Walks linked with bus routes are described in local bus timetables while the National Trust also publishes details of suggested walks on their land.

The South West Coast Path, immortalised in Mark Wallington's book, *Five Hundred Mile Walkies*, begins at Minehead and runs for 500 miles around the south-west peninsula to Studland Bay in Dorset. Some guidebooks describe the whole route while the NPA publishes a guide to the section of the path between Minehead and Combe Martin. It breaks the walk into sections with alternative return routes forming long and short circular walks. Full details from ENP Visitor Centres.

There is open access to much of Exmoor and the experienced walker may want to work out his or her own route. The best maps to use are the Ordnance Survey Outdoor Leisure Map 9 (Exmoor) and the OS Landranger Map sheet 180.

For those who feel a little uncertain of venturing on their own there is a full programme of guided walks arranged in spring, summer and autumn. Some are led by National Park staff and others by experienced volunteers. Many of these specialise in some particular aspect of Exmoor – the coast, birds, archaeological features and so on. Details of these guided walks can be found in the *Exmoor Visitor*, at ENP Visitor Centres and Village Information Agencies.

If you are really going to enjoy walking on Exmoor it is worth being properly equipped. This doesn't necessarily mean expensive gear. For most Exmoor walks sensible stout shoes with a good grip are quite adequate although proper walking boots are a worth-while investment if you intend to walk on the wetter moorland areas. It is always advisable to take an additional warm sweater and a waterproof in case of bad weather. It's probably more important to be warm than dry and beware of flimsy nylon anoraks which keep you neither warm nor dry!

TICKS

Ticks are a fact of life in the countryside and some can carry infections like Lyme Disease. These tiny spider-like creatures attach themselves to passing animals and people and feed by biting through the skin and sucking blood. A bite can affect the skin and sometimes cause complications and serious illness. It's important to take precautions when walking on the moor or in woodland. Keep your skin covered. Wear trousers and long sleeved shirts and shoes not sandals. A leaflet with more details is available from ENP Visitor Centres.

NB If you are intending to go for a long walk it is sensible to tell someone where you are going and what time you expect to return.

THE COUNTRY CODE

• Respect the life of the countryside and the people who live there.

• Guard against all risks of fire.

• If you open a gate make sure you shut it firmly behind you.

• Make sure your dog is under control at all times.

• Keep to the public path especially when walking through farmland.

• Use gates and stiles to cross fences, hedges and walls to avoid damaging them.

• Leave livestock, crops and machinery alone.

• Always take your litter home.

• Help to keep water clean.

• Protect wildlife, plants and trees.

• Take special care on country roads.

• Make no unnecessary noise.

RIDING AND TREKKING

Riding in all its forms is Exmoor's chief sport and it's not surprising that the area has been described as the 'riding playground of England'. Certainly there can be few better ways of viewing Exmoor, for the rider can see over the hedges and enjoy the scenery while the horse concentrates on where it is putting its feet! With a 644km (400 mile) network of bridleways in the National Park across open moorland, through wooded combes and valleys and by clear streams and rivers, the possibilities are endless.

There are riding centres across Exmoor which cater for everyone from beginner to experienced rider. There are facilities for hunting, hacking, jumping and trekking while several hotels and guest houses provide stabling as well. Some establishments offer complete riding holidays, including accommodation and instruction. Children are welcome at most stables while some cater especially for school and youth groups. A list of riding establishments can be found in the *Exmoor Visitor*.

Every sort of ride is available from a gentle couple of hours escorted amble for the beginner to a hard day's ride for the

Wading through the ford at Tarr Steps

E. R. J. Davey

dedicated. Don't worry if you have no kit. Most stables provide hard hats, which should always be worn. No other special wear is necessary although a waterproof anorak, trousers and stout shoes are helpful. Walking boots or wellingtons are not recommended as they can be trapped in the stirrups, but it is always sensible to take waterproofs with you.

Many local clubs, societies and hunts arrange competitive events such as point-to-points, gymkhanas and shows throughout the year which are advertised in the local press and Exmoor is also the venue for the Golden Horseshoe Ride, an internationally renowned two-day endurance event.

CYCLING

CYCLING OFFROAD
Exmoor is a landscape of great contrast and beauty. Thickly wooded combes rising to wild, open moorland and the numerous bridleways and forest tracks all make for some really exciting offroad cycling. Although offroad cycling is permitted on all bridleways it can sometimes prove a hazard to walkers and horse riders so cyclists are encouraged to use the routes specially prepared for them. These include routes for riders of varying experience and abilities, including families, in Dunster Woods and in the vicinity of Wimbleball Lake (ENP leaflets available) and also on Selworthy Hill. (NT leaflet)

CYCLING ONROAD
Many of Exmoor's quiet roads provide good routes for cycling particularly where there are wide verges and where the gradi-

A family outing on Winsford Hill

ents are not too steep. Cycles can be hired in Barnstaple and Minehead.

Part of the National Cycle Network developed by Sustrans crosses southern Exmoor, passing through Brushford and Dulverton with a steep climb up towards West Anstey and following the ridge road over towards Mole's Chamber and Bratton Fleming. Many people have commented that this is one of the best parts of the route. Details from the ENP Visitor Centre at Dulverton.

CYCLING CODE
By following this basic code you will help to give mountain bikers the image they properly deserve.

• Ride only on permitted routes

• Do not make undue noise

• Give way to walkers and horses

• Announce your presence when approaching walkers or riders from the rear

• Take care not to drop litter or start fires

• Minimize your impact on the environment by avoiding excessively worn tracks especially during wet weather

• Brake sensibly

• Close gates behind you

• Follow the Country Code

• Beware of forestry operations

ON THE WATER

FISHING – FRESHWATER
Exmoor is a paradise for game fishermen although lack of rain at certain times of year recently has meant a corresponding lack of water in the rivers and a limitation of the sport. The Exe, Barle and East Lyn are traditional salmon rivers while sea trout also run up the East Lyn as well as the Avill. These and rivers

E. R. J. Davey

At Wimbleball

such as the West Lyn, Oare Water, Horner Water, Haddeo, Mole and Bray provide good fly fishing for brown trout. Most moorland streams contain brown trout, and although smaller the fish provide good sport and tasty eating. All Exmoor rivers are spate streams, rapidly varying in volume and speed according to the amount of rain or snow melt, and one can expect a variety of conditions for fishing.

Two reservoirs in the National Park – Wimbleball and Nutscale – provide good fly-fishing for trout as do Slade, Wistlandpound and Clatworthy reservoirs nearby. Most still water fisheries require a licence and in many cases an owner's permit as well. Details of where to obtain licences and permits can be found in the *Exmoor Visitor* or from ENP Visitor Centres.

FISHING – SEAWATER

There is really good sea fishing from Exmoor's beaches and harbours all the year round. Catches include cod, whiting, bass, conger, skate, mackerel, the occasional shark and the inevitable dogfish.

Access to beaches is limited. Bossington beach, near Porlock, is very popular as is the stretch of road above the beach at Blue Anchor just outside the National Park. From Minehead,

Combe Martin, Lynmouth, Porlock Weir, Watchet and Ilfracombe licensed fishing boats take groups along the coast. Tackle and bait can be provided and, as the boat owners know the area, the chance of a catch is that much greater. Arrangements to hire a boat or join a fishing trip can usually be made at the harbours mentioned.

SAILING AND SURFING

Sailing off the Exmoor coast is popular but very limited by tides in the Bristol Channel. The strong currents and local conditions dictate the times when sailing is possible, particularly where launching and landing are concerned.

The usual points of access are Combe Martin, Lynmouth, Porlock Weir and Minehead. Local advice should be sought and attention paid to the weather forecast before putting to sea. It is not uncommon for sailors unfamiliar with the area to discover that they are unable to return on the same tide, and then have to sit it out or be towed back or – worse still – rescued.

E. R. J. Davey

Porlock Weir

Inland there is good safe sailing on Wimbleball Lake controlled by the Wimbleball Sailing Club. Board-sailing and canoeing are also possible here.

Surfing is sometimes possible at Lynmouth when there is a strong northerly wind, but the Atlantic beaches at Croyde and Woolacombe are more suitable. There you can hire surfboards and also receive instruction if you want it.

SWIMMING

There are no sandy beaches within the boundaries of the National Park although there are several nearby. Access to beaches is often restricted by high cliffs while strong currents make bathing unsafe near headlands. It is therefore wise to stay close to the shore when bathing. Make sure you check tide times as well.

Probably the most popular beach is Lee Bay near Lynton. This is accessible via the Lee Abbey toll road and there is a car park nearby. Also suitable for bathing are Woody Bay, Wringcliff Bay (near the Valley of Rocks) and Wild Pear Beach at Combe Martin though access to all of these places involves long walks and steep climbs.

There are public swimming pools at Ilfracombe, Barnstaple, South Molton, Tiverton and Minehead.

WATCHING WILDLIFE

Many people come to Exmoor hoping to see Red Deer, Exmoor Ponies, merlins and buzzards. Inevitably some leave disappointed for it is impossible to guarantee seeing certain animals and birds. However, armed with a little knowledge it is possible to increase one's chances.

It helps a lot to know the habits of the creatures one is looking for and where they are likely to be found. For instance, many animals are nocturnal and even those which are not may not be active during the middle of the day. Early morning and late evening are good times to watch for most creatures.

Deer spend much of the day in woodland but may come out in the open to graze in the evening and early morning. The time to watch for them on open moorland is early summer when the

young grasses are most palatable. In winter they're more often seen on the fringes of farmland while they may be found at any time in woodland. It's important to train oneself to look for them and recognise them when you see them as they are well camouflaged against the moorland and sometimes appear to be farm animals which they often graze near.

Exmoor Ponies are easier to find though not all ponies to be seen on Exmoor are pure-bred. There are pure-bred Exmoor herds on Withypool Common, Winsford Hill, Dunkery Hill and Porlock Common while the National Park Authority has small herds on Haddon Hill and Warren.

Birds that you can be sure of seeing are the seabirds which nest on the cliffs at Woody Bay and the Valley of Rocks but to do so a boat is indispensable. In the summer regular boat trips ply from Lynmouth and Combe Martin especially to see the birds.

There are plenty of people to help you watch and identify wildlife. The Exmoor Natural History Society has a field centre at Malmsmead which is open to the public at certain times

Red Deer camouflaged against the bracken

during the year and guided walks are provided by their members. A full programme of walks from April to October is arranged by ENP staff and many of these specialise in aspects of Exmoor's natural history. Full listings can be found in the *Exmoor Visitor*. There are also a number of commercial organisations that lead groups over the moor specifically to see Red Deer.

There are several inexpensive pictorial guides on the market which are useful for the amateur interested in identifying plants and birds.

HIT THE TRADITION

Three traditional customs are carried out today on Exmoor with verve and style. If you are around at the right time it's well worth making the effort to join in.

Musical events throughout the year on Exmoor range from classical music to jazz to folk music. Details of regular meetings of folk clubs and of special courses and workshops can be obtained from Folk SouthWest, The Stables, Montacute House, Montacute, Somerset. TA15 6XP. 01935 822911. Other musical and artistic events in the area are advertised in the *Exmoor Visitor* and the local press but details can be obtained in advance from the Arts Coordinator, West Somerset District Council, Williton, Somerset (01984 632291) and the Arts Officer, North Devon District Council (01271 327711).

Minehead Hobby Horse dances out on May Day and successive days. Here the Hobby Horse with its attendant gullivers and musicians is 'booting' a victim about one hundred years ago.

Wassailing the apple trees to ensure a good crop takes place each year in Carhampton on 17 January in the evening. Toast soaked in cider is placed in the branches of the trees for the robins, or good spirits, while guns are fired to frighten the evil spirits away. The traditional Carhampton wassail song is sung.

Caroline Shipsey

The ceremony of the Hunting of the Earl of Rone at Combe Martin takes place over the May Bank holiday weekend, with a series of street processions, music, dancing, a hobby horse and fool and the eventual seeking out and capture of the 'Earl'. The street procession on the final night is led by a woman carrying a ribboned stick and the principal dancers carrying a flower-bedecked rope.

E. R. J. Davey

David Manners

Judging Exmoor Horns at Dunster Show

SHOWS AND FESTIVALS

During the summer months there are plenty of opportunities to enjoy a day out at a show or village fete, highlights of the year for local people. At agricultural shows like that at Dunster on the third Friday in August, you can see Exmoor's farming at its best with prize sheep and cattle on show as well as riding and jumping competitions. Exmoor Ponies are shown at Exford Show while many villages celebrate annually with fêtes often including flower shows, stalls, games and refreshments. Earlier in the year there are exciting point-to-points where local riders and horses compete over the hurdles. Visitors are always welcome at these events which give them the opportunity to mingle with Exmoor folk.

A TASTE OF EXMOOR

If you enjoy eating out and sampling traditional specialities, or buying local fresh ingredients for a meal back in the cottage or caravan, Exmoor has plenty to offer.

Cream teas are first favourite and it won't be long before you identify your favourite teashop or farmhouse where the scones are freshly baked just to your liking and bowls are heaped with clotted cream and jam. If the jam has been made from whortle-berries or 'worts' then your joy should be complete. Worts are tiny purplish-blue berries, known elsewhere as bilberries or blaeberries, which ripen on the moor in July. Occasionally you may see the berries on sale or you could pick your own but it is a back-breaking job. Better perhaps to buy a jar of locally-made whortleberry jam to take home. Clotted cream used to be made in every farmhouse, using milk from the house cow, and sold at the door but now rules and regulations govern its production. However it is still possible to buy clotted cream to be posted to your friends at home.

Exmoor is farming country and the farmers are rightly proud of the quality of their produce. Exmoor-reared beef, lamb and pork is first-rate and many local butchers advertise the sources of their meat. Fresh seafish including crab, lobster and mack-erel often features on restaurant menus while local trout and related products are on sale at a number of trout farms. A deli-cacy from the seashore is laver, a kind of seaweed, which can be bought potted, or fresh in the autumn.

Whortleberries

objects in wood, pottery and glass; jewellery; textiles and leather goods are all created on Exmoor in small workshops, sometimes using local materials. Many workshops are open for you to visit though you may need to make an appointment. The Exmoor Producers' Association publishes a guide to craft workshops that welcome visitors and shops where local products are sold. It is available at ENP Visitor Centres and includes a map to help you locate some of the places that are off the beaten track.

All the year round but especially in the summer months there are exhibitions of the work of local artists. These are advertised in the local press and are well worth visiting. Often there are paintings or photographs of Exmoor scenes for sale while at Dunster, in the shop and showroom of the Somerset Guild of Craftsmen, the work of several Exmoor artists and makers can be seen.

Locally-produced cheeses and free-range eggs can be obtained across the moor while a visit to the pannier markets at South Molton and Barnstaple will provide the opportunity to buy fresh fruit and vegetables picked that very morning as well as dairy goods. Delicious cakes, chocolates, ice cream, cider: the list of local produce is endless. Many producers belong to the Exmoor Producers' Association whose publicity leaflets will help you source these goodies. Food is always a welcome present and honey, preserves, cheese and stoneground flour are all easy to transport.

MADE ON EXMOOR

When you are looking for a souvenir to take home to remind you of your holiday why not choose something produced by one of Exmoor's many talented artists and makers. Beautiful

Craft demonstration at Wimbleball Open Day 1998

WHERE TO GO AND WHAT TO SEE

HISTORIC SITES AND BUILDINGS
(see also villages)

Arlington Court SS 611 405 Refreshments Shop 01271 850296
National Trust property in North Devon. Open to public. Once
the home of the Chichester family. Furnished Regency house.
Collections of model ships, shells, pewter and horse-drawn
carriages. Walks and carriage rides in extensive grounds with
gardens, park and lake.

Bat's Castle SS 988 422 ENP walk: Gallox Hill, Dunster
Iron Age fort with wonderful views towards Dunkery and
across the Bristol Channel. Nearby is a smaller hill-slope enclosure.

Beulah Chapel ST 027 343
Old Bible Christian mining chapel at an isolated road junction
in the Brendon Hills, one mile west of Raleigh's Cross. Weekly
service.

Burgundy Chapel SS 947 482
Ruined chapel or hermitage built c.1500 perhaps to fulfil a vow
made during a time of great peril. On National Park
Authority's North Hill estate and can be reached via footpath
from Minehead harbour.

Burrow Farm Engine House ST 007 345
Approached by a footpath which runs beside the old discon-
tinued mineral line, the ruined engine house marks the site of
the Burrow Farm iron mine. See Raleigh's Cross.

Caractacus Stone SS 890 335
Inscribed stone from the Dark Ages (c.450) in a stone shelter
near Spire Cross on Winsford Hill.

Clicket SS 962 397
Deserted and ruined hamlet in the Brendon Hills two miles
south of Timerscombe. Best reached by footpath from road
between Dunster and Luxborough.

Burrow Hill Engine House

E. R. J. Davey

Cleeve Abbey ST 047 407 Shop 01984 640377
Fine remains of Cistercian abbey near village of Washford. In
the care of English Heritage and open to the public all year
round.

Cow Castle SS 795 373 ENP Walk leaflet: Barle Valley,
Simonsbath
Iron Age fort on natural hillock in Barle Valley. Can be reached
by walking up from Landacre Bridge or down from
Simonsbath on marked footpaths.

Culbone SS 843 483
Tiny hamlet set in deep shaded valley. The ancient church is
said to be the smallest parish church in England. There is no

Culbone Church

Dunster Castle

public road leading to Culbone which is best reached by footpath from Porlock Weir.

Dunster Castle SS 990 437 CP NT 01643 821314 Shop.
Original medieval castle reconstructed in 19th century. Gardens.

Five Barrows SS 733 368
A prominent hill 493m (1619ft) three miles SE of Simonsbath. There are actually nine Bronze Age burial mounds including a bell barrow on private moorland.

Heasley Mill SS 735 323
Small hamlet in the Mole Valley. Centre of mining activity in the nineteenth century. Some derelict buildings and spoil heaps remain.

Larkbarrow SS 820 429
A ruined Knight farm on the moorland track from Larkbarrow Gate near Alderman's Barrow to Badgworthy Water. Part of the ENPA's estate.

Longstone SS 705 431
Finest of Exmoor's Bronze Age standing stones 9ft (3m) high. On a wet and desolate part of the moor between Wood Barrow and Chapmans Barrows.

Luckwell Bridge SS 905 387
Hamlet between Exford and Wheddon Cross in the parish of Cutcombe. The bridge is over the River Quarme. In 1830 there were two mills here. The name refers to St Luke's Well which is now covered over.

Pinkworthy Pond SS 724 424
Pronounced Pinkery, this pond was created by damming the head waters of the River Barle in about 1830. It was built for the landowner John Knight but its purpose isn't clear for the pond and its associated canal system were never used. It is now owned by ENPA and is best approached by footpath from the B3358 between Challacombe and Simonsbath.

Raleigh's Cross ST 039 344 Inn
On Brendon Hills with inn of long-standing. Once centre of iron mining industry. Remains of old miner's cottages and other related buildings and the top of the mineral railway

incline can be seen on private land one mile west. See also Burrow Farm Engine House.

Tarr Steps SS 868 322 CP ($^1/_2$mile) PC Refreshments
Narrow approach roads can be very congested at peak times which are best avoided.
Ancient causeway over the River Barle. Fine example of a clapper bridge but age is unknown.

Whitstones SS 853 464
Two ancient stones near the top of Porlock Hill. Legend says they were thrown there in a contest between the Devil and a giant.

PLACES TO VISIT IN THE COUNTRYSIDE

Alderman's Barrow SS 837 423
Bronze Age burial mound by roadside four miles north of Exford. Once a boundary mark of the Royal Forest. A good starting point for walks over the ENPA's Larkbarrow Estate.

Badgworthy Water SS 792 497 CP PC Refreshments in locality ENP Moorland Walk leaflet: Doone Country and Doone Country walk booklet
This lovely valley is best known for its association with the story of Lorna Doone. The most popular approach is from Malmsmead but roads are narrow and can be congested at peak times. Alternative approach from County Gate.

Bossington SS 898 478 CP PC Refreshments
Pretty hamlet mainly owned by the National Trust. Good starting point for walks on Bossington Hill and Porlock Bay. Shingle ridge and lagoon. NT walks leaflets available

Brendon Two Gates SS 765 433
Modern cattle grid on Simonsbath to Lynton road (B3223) now bridges gap in the old Knight wall once closed by a double gate. Good starting point for walks eastwards down Hoccombe Water or westwards towards the Hoar Oak Tree following the county boundary. To the north-east on Brendon Common is a memorial to Col. R.H. Maclaren killed on duty here in 1941.

The Chains SS 735 418
The map reference is for Chains Barrow 487m (1597ft), highest point on Exmoor's central wilderness of waterlogged deer sedge and purple moor grass. Here the rivers Exe, Barle and West Lyn rise. Approach either via Pinkworthy Pond (easiest) or from Brendon Two Gates via Hoar Oak Tree and Long Chains Combe.

Cloutsham SS 892 431
Farm, stream and woodland to the north of Dunkery belonging to the National Trust. Popular for walks and picnics. Narrow roads can get congested. Approach on foot from Horner or Webber's Post.

County Gate SS 794 487 CP PC VC
Where the A39 coast road crosses the Somerset/Devon boundary. ENP Visitor Centre (open Easter to October). Fine views over the Bristol Channel and across the East Lyn valley to Doone country. Good starting point for walks to the Glenthorne estate and Doone country.

Croydon Hill SS 975 405
Forested part of the Brendon Hills crossed by Dunster to Luxborough road. Highest point 381m (1250ft). Fine views from nearby Black Hill. Parking and picnic area.

Looking towards Dunkery Beacon

E. R. J. Davey

Culbone SS 843 483
Tiny hamlet with ancient church set in woods best reached by footpath from Porlock Weir.

Doone Country The setting of R.D. Blackmore's *Lorna Doone*. An ENP booklet *A Doone Country Walk* summarises the story. The walk visits sites mentioned in the book. Start from County Gate, Middle Hill or Malmsmead. See also Badgworthy Water and Malmsmead.

Dunkery Beacon SS 891 416
The highest point 519m (1704ft) on Exmoor (and in Somerset), where fire beacons were, and are, lit. Part of the National Trust Holnicote Estate. Extensive views of up to thirteen counties on clear days.

Exe Head SS 752 413
Source of River Exe in boggy ground 457m up on the eastern edge of the Chains.

Foreland Point SS 755 510
Exmoor's most northerly point owned by the National Trust. Precipitous cliffs and footpath to lighthouse.

Grabbist SS 980 435
Part of a four-mile range of hills rising to 295m (970ft) between Dunster and Tivington. Extensive views to Dunkery, Brendon Hills and over Minehead and the Bristol Channel.

Great Hangman SS 600 480
At 318m (1044ft) part of a range of hills and hogs-backed cliffs between Combe Martin and the sea. Owned by the National Trust and crossed by the South West Coast Path.

Hawkcombe SS 885 462
Hamlet and valley near Porlock. Once had a flourishing woollen industry. Walk along Hawkcombe Water through old woodlands belonging to the ENPA.

Heddon's Mouth SS 655 497
Deep valley and small beach at mouth of River Heddon. Reached by mile-long footpath from Hunter's Inn. (National Trust leaflet)

Hoar Oak Tree SS 748 430
Ancient boundary mark of Exmoor Forest near former Knight estate wall by Hoaroak Water. The present tree, the third in more than 300 years, was planted in 1917. Follow the wall westwards from Brendon Two Gates over 2 miles of hilly country.

Horner SS 899 454 CP PC
Cluster of houses in Luccombe parish near Horner Water at the foot of Dunkery, part of the National Trust Holnicote Estate. Its name is said to have come from the Saxon 'hwrnwr' – the snorer – on account of the gurgling stream. Picturesque walks beside the water through ancient woodland to Cloutsham or Webber's Post.

Hurlstone Point SS 898 494
Easterly point of Porlock Bay. Interesting area for marine biology but rocks can be hazardous and beware the incoming tide.

Landacre Bridge SS 816 362
Well-preserved medieval bridge over the River Barle near Withypool Common. Popular picnic area. Walks up-river towards Cow Castle Iron Age fort and Simonsbath.

Landacre Bridge

E. R. J. Davey

Malmsmead SS 791 477 CP PC Refreshments Shop ENP walk: Doone Country
Hamlet on Badgworthy Water near where it joins Oare Water to form the East Lyn River. Easiest starting point for walks in Doone Country. Exmoor Natural History Society field centre open mid-week in summer. Roads become congested so avoid peak times.

North Hill SS 940 478
Immediately to the west of Minehead overlooking the town and Bristol Channel. Former military road past Selworthy Beacon is now a fine scenic drive. Plenty of easy walking.

Robber's Bridge SS 820 465 CP
Small and narrow stone bridge over Weir Water. Favourite picnic site. Starting point for walks.

Robin How SS 908 428
One of a group of Bronze Age barrows (burial mounds) giving its name to a part of Dunkery Hill. The road from Webber's Post to Dunkery Hill Gate climbs between Robin How 428m (1404ft)and Dunkery Beacon 519m (1704ft).

Robber's Bridge

Valley of Rocks SS 705 496 CP PC Refreshments
Unusual streamless valley, a mile west of Lynton. Fascinating rock formations such as Chimney Rock, Castle Rock, Rugged Jack and Devil's Cheesewring. Can be approached on foot along South West Coast Path from Lynmouth.

Watersmeet SS 744 487 Refreshments (S) Shop NT information centre
ENP Walk leaflet: Watersmeet
19th century fishing lodge (NT) where East Lyn river and Hoar Oak Water meet. Starting point for beautiful walks on signed footpaths.

Watersmeet

PLACES TO TAKE THE FAMILY

Allerford Museum
Open from Good Friday until the end of October
This museum of West Somerset Rural Life includes plenty of things to interest the family. Exhibits show how Exmoor people used to live and work. Children can compare the Victorian schoolroom with its original desks and forms,

slates and toys with their own classroom. Special activities on occasion, a cobbler's workshop and a riverside picnic area.

Lynton and Lynmouth

There is plenty for the family to do in Lynton and Lynmouth including a journey from one village to the other by the water-powered Cliff Railway (though if you are not fond of heights you may prefer to walk!). For running times see the *Exmoor Visitor*.

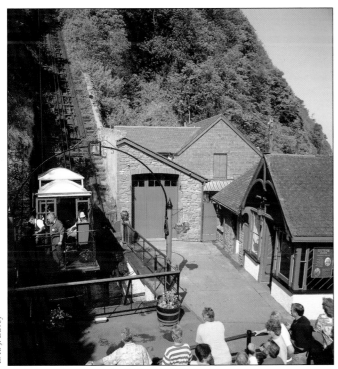

Lynton and Lynmouth Cliff Railway

Malmsmead Field Centre CP behind Lorna Doone Farm (SS 792 478) Open some afternoons in summer. Check times in the *Exmoor Visitor*.
Exmoor Natural History Society Field Centre houses fascinating displays about Exmoor's wildlife. Picnic area, pond and an area of rough grass frequented by butterflies. Children's activity sheets available.

Nutcombe Bottom, near Dunster CP
Play and picnic area situated in woodland. Access for disabled people. Starting point for walks and bike rides. Crown Estate guide leaflets available.

West Somerset Railway

Go for a nostalgic journey on the West Somerset Railway. Trains, often drawn by steam locomotives, run all the year round from Minehead to Bishop's Lydeard and back. There are plenty of stops en route so that you can visit the seaside at Blue Anchor or Watchet or other attractions along the way. More detail from the West Somerset Railway Station, Minehead. TA24 5BG. 01643 704996. Talking timetable 01643 707650

West Somerset Railway

Wimbleball Lake

This reservoir is surrounded by woodland and meadow and provides facilities for walking, picnicking, nature study, sailing, fishing and camping. It is an excellent place to take the children; refreshments are available in the summer and there is plenty of space to run about, play games and explore. There is an infants' play centre and a rustic trail for the more adventurous. A Nature Reserve has a self-guided nature trail. More information from ENP Visitor Centres.

WHERE TO FIND OUT MORE

EXMOOR NATIONAL PARK VISITOR CENTRES

The Centres are open from Easter until the end of September with limited opening at Dunster and Dulverton during the winter. For opening times see the *Exmoor Visitor*.

Combe Martin
Seacot, Cross Street
01271 883319

County Gate
A39 Countisbury
01598 741321

Dulverton
Fore Street
01398 323841

Dunster
Dunster Steep
01643 821835

Lynmouth
The Esplanade
01598 752509

VILLAGE INFORMATION AGENCIES

These local shops and post offices are happy to advise on walk routes and hold a stock of ENP information leaflets. While you make your enquiry why not buy something for your picnic, evening meal or a present of local goods to take home.

Allerford Post Office
Barbrook Post Office
Brompton Regis Post Office and Stores
Challacombe Post Office
Parracombe Stores and Post Office

Allerford Post Office

Wheddon Cross Post Office and Stores
Winsford Stores and Post Office
Withypool Post Office and Stores
Wootton Courtenay: The Villagers' Stores

MUSEUMS

Most museums are only open in the summer. Check times in the *Exmoor Visitor*.

Allerford Museum, The Old School, Allerford, Minehead, Somerset TA24 8HN Exhibits and old photographs feature rural life in West Somerset. Victorian schoolroom, cobbler's workshop and riverside picnic area.

Combe Martin Museum, 4 Kingsley Terrace, Combe Martin, Devon EX34 0EW
Old village industries, agriculture, horticulture and maritime history. Guided tours of key industrial sites can be arranged.

Dovery Manor Museum, High Street, Porlock.
Changing displays feature Porlock parish artefacts, photographs and press cuttings. Activities for children.

Guildhall Heritage Centre, Monmouth Terrace, Dulverton
Small museum of Dulverton 100 years ago.
Exmoor Photographic Archive is held here.

Lyn and Exmoor Museum, St Vincent's Cottage, Market Street, Lynton. EX35 6AF
Includes Exmoor kitchen, agricultural tools and implements, archaeological and geological displays. Model of Lynton/Barnstaple railway, closed 1935.

Dovery Manor Museum, Porlock

South Molton Museum, Town Hall, The Square, South Molton, Devon EX36 3AB
Depicts the life and times of the town and surrounding area.

Watchet Museum, Market Street, Watchet TA23 0AN
Features the history of Watchet, sailors and sailing vessels and the Brendon Hill iron mines and mineral railway.

GUIDED WALKS AND LECTURES

These are arranged throughout the year and are lead by ENP staff and qualified volunteers. Full listings can be found in the *Exmoor Visitor*.

FREE PUBLICATIONS FROM EXMOOR NATIONAL PARK AUTHORITY

The Exmoor National Park Authority's *Services* booklet explains how they can help both local people and visitors in all sorts of ways. It includes background information and useful addresses.
Exmoor Visitor is published annually, can be found in outlets all over Exmoor and is full of up-to-date information, listings and advertisements.
Park Life is published twice a year and circulated to people living within the Park. It reports on the activities of the Park Authority. The *Annual Report* describes the work of the Park Authority in the previous year.

SOCIETIES CONCERNED WITH EXMOOR

The **Exmoor Society** is an action group that cares for Exmoor and works to conserve and promote its unique value as a National Park. For further details contact the Exmoor Society, Parish Rooms, Dulverton. TA22 9DP 01398 323335

The **Exmoor Natural History Society** exists to study and record the flora and fauna of Exmoor and make that information available to the public. Caroline Giddens 01643 707624

The **Exmoor Pony Society** exists to promote and encourage the breeding of pure-bred Exmoor Ponies. Further information from Exmoor House, Dulverton TA22 9HL 01398 323665 or the Exmoor Pony Society, Glen Fern, Waddicombe, Dulverton TA22 9RY. 01398 341490

FURTHER READING

Allen, N.V., *Churches and Chapels of Exmoor*, The Exmoor Press, 1974

Ed. Atkinson, Michael, *Exmoor's Industrial Archaeology*, Exmoor Books, 1997

Binding, H , *Discovering Dunster*, Exmoor Press, 1990

Bonham-Carter, V., *The Essence of Exmoor*, The Exmoor Press, 1991

Burton, S.H., *Exmoor*, Westaway Books, 1952

Bourne, H.L., *A Little History of Exmoor*, Dent, 1968

Burton, R.A., *The Heritage of Exmoor*, Pp, 1989

Burton, R.A., *Simonsbath*, Pp, 1984

Grinsell, L.V., *The Archaeology of Exmoor*, David and Charles, 1970

Eardley-Wilmot, H., *Ancient Exmoor*, Exmoor Press, 1983

Eardley-Wilmot, H., *Yesterday's Exmoor*, Exmoor Books, 1990

Gilman, John, *Exmoor's Maritime Heritage*, Exmoor Books, 1999

Grinsell. L.V., *The Archaeology of Exmoor*, David and Charles, 1970

Hurley, J., *Legends of Exmoor*, Exmoor Press, 1980

Lawrence, Berta, *Exmoor Villages*, Exmoor Press, 1984

Orwin, C,S. *The Reclamation of Exmoor Forest* (revised Sellick, R.J. David and Charles, 1970 and Bonham-Carter, V. Exmoor Books, 1997)

Sellick, R.J. *The Old Mineral Line*, Exmoor Press

PERIODICALS

Exmoor Naturalist, annually from the Exmoor Natural History Society

Exmoor Review, annually from the Exmoor Society

Exmoor – The Country Magazine, quarterly. On sale throughout Exmoor. In case of difficulty ring 01884 243242.

E. R. J. Davey